Brooklyn
(the black)

Brooklyn
(the black)

a memoir by Asha Veal Brisebois

THE PLACES WE'VE BEEN BOOKS
Chicago

For Joseph, whom I hadn't met yet

KuSandra and Martin
Aunt De

A version of "Sputnik" was originally published online in 2009 by Slice Literary.
A version of "Yuko" was originally published online in 2009 by Slice Literary.

ISBN (hardcover): 978-0-9890389-7-3
ISBN (paperback): 978-0-9890389-8-0

Library of Congress Control Number: 2015931415

Biography & Autobiography: Personal Memoirs
Poetry: Women Authors
Poetry: American – African American

Note: Some names and identifying details have been changed to protect the privacy of individuals.

Published by:

The Places We've Been books / The Places We've Been, LLC
Chicago, IL
www.theplaces35.com
www.facebook.com/ThePlaces35

Book design and cover by: The Places We've Been books

First edition, 2015

10 9 8 7 6 5 4 3 2 1

THANKS AND ACKNOWLEDGMENTS

to Everybody.

especially C. James, J. Nguyen, F. Rahman, L. Sentz.

plus A. Threatt, A. Phillips Threatt, B. Williams, J. Oliver,
A. Naidoo, M. Dorsey, E. Choice, L. Kass, A. Patterson.

honor and remembrance to T. Spann, C. Leonard,
B. Cerile, B. Sutton, E. Tidwell, I. Turner.

always D. Curry and J. Curry.

*A lion is the crouch and the bristle and the roar that my body bulks out into...
when I am hungry and strong, watching one stranger pitter patter all over my
territory—right before I eat him up.*

—Ascia Vitello, 2005

*It can't just be the same people writing about race all the time. We need to
hear from new people—especially young people who have grown up with the
whole notion of multiculturalism.*

—Hettie Jones, 2007

I. Brooklyn (the Black) / 2004 through 2006

Brooklyn.

Me and all my friends just moved to Brooklyn. We walked far out of New York City central and over the bridge, either moving into brownstone apartments or artist buildings across the street from city projects.

My own first home in that borough stood three floors up at the center of a mixed Afro-Caribbean and black Islamic neighborhood, next door to a storefront mosque. Dark men in airy clothes bowed down on grit-stained concrete while a loudspeaker echoed their prayer out for the entire neighborhood to hear.

A street sign on that block's southeastern corner stood as the only marker of where one of the world's most famous and notoriously plump, now dead rappers, used to alternate between trading rhymes and taking money for drugs, ten years prior to when my South Korean roommates' father bought the small building so we could move in.

In that first Brooklyn bedroom without a window, my eyes opened up in the dark and under wind from a ceiling fan, popped open by the adult child one floor below. Every morning we felt him whoop and taz like he wanted to break free of his own mind and the inside of that tiny apartment.

Behind their front door, that family's father ate dinner with two wives. Down our shared stairwell, my bare legs like jointed cinnamon sticks walked up, down, out from underneath big flower sundresses and tiger faced T-shirts, more suggestive of me as a softly scented, physically unaware girl, than of a grown lady intentionally playing upon whatever the unveiled powers of this new womanhood may be.

Like shoes. Eighty-five pairs of kicks on three silver racks outside our front door told on me and my ladies as not being "made in Brooklyn" originals, worried about our dancing heels or street sneakers getting stolen. A black American girl with two Long Island Koreans. We ate Halal buffet and bean pies from the immigrant African Arabs to the left. We ordered vegetable rice and deep-fried chicken wings from the Chinese takeout on the right. One block over, we shopped for food at our neighborhood's big grocery store, the one where black music played from speakers tracked along the ceiling. Black like me and de la hip hop, black like a beat to turn around.

The older West Indian ladies on checkout at the store liked to fondly call me Sis. Those grown women curved over onto countertops and arched sideways against register doors, like island flamingos or crane birds held back from flying up by apron strings of blue. A pink Arab bouncer watched over us all. He sat daily at his post by the exit door, baggy jean legs spread wide apart on either side of an overturned milk crate.

Most everyone felt at home together in this Brooklyn mottle of cultures and cool.

But after six long months here in Brooklyn, the non-visible spaces inside of my head must look like a diorama of war: so many elements filled with fire and raging, that used to whirl lovely and easy to the song of a beautiful dream.

And even though they shake up my body and rock hard against the always and ever before knowledge of my mind, colored explosions against a black scene do look beautiful.

I remember the blackened soles of mine and my friends' naked feet, acquired on dirty, humid summer nights spent atop tarred and sanded, Brooklyn apartment rooftops. An alternating collection of friends to share a four-dollar bottle of wine.

A literary ballerina and her Texas Australian roommate became my fabulous cohorts in making a plan to run away from daytime to a magical adventure life. We hung out over an Iranian hookah lounge where shadowy strangers breathed in deep over sweet leaves, and pressed lips against lips like the gluey bellies of snails.

Bette the ballerina showed me an old-fashioned typewriter now used for writing detective stories. Sarah the Texas Australian talked a lot about confidence, that stolen-back power we used to all have but for some time now in this new Brooklyn life has gone away missing. Me, the virgin, worked full-time in Manhattan for a playwright best known for her show about the life experiences of individual vaginas.

I imagine a memory of my friend Bette sitting next to a window on a southbound commuter train, the day when she left the boroughs for a weekend. This graceful girl who walks clumsy and keeps little round bandages on the tops of her toes. My friend hit her face, walked right into a sliding door, then licked tongue against teeth to feel a chipped tooth.

Last week my friends ran into a girl we used to know during school who now has one gold incisor.

Bette promised that she'll get a porcelain. Gold might actually better match the BBQ restaurant where she waits tables, but then would leave the other ballerinas a little in shock.

My friend traveled home to fix her tooth and audition for a company. She got accepted and left the borough forever for Tennessee.

Our last time all together, we stared down from a rooftop at the twinkle of what we knew as urban fireflies, the white fluorescent bulbs and lights that lined restaurant patios and terraces below.

But sometimes bad things happened in Brooklyn, so maintaining a champion's life became tougher when we all moved out here.

Like that Saturday night sitting outside on a street curb at lower 7th, beside my friend in a bold gold dress and tears falling down her face. Cars and cabs passed far too fast and far too close to our noses and feet, while a million lights shimmered on the pavement. My friend's sister earlier got stuck in the back of the hand with a needle.

"We don't know the HIV status of the blood that was in the needle."

Sometimes in Brooklyn, friends took care of each other because families lived too far away. Or because mothers and fathers are harder to ask a question like,

"Does it count as rape if—"

He broke his promise to her, pinched two fingers around his penis, and slid the condom off to come.

Or in an entirely separate case—

She woke up nauseated and asked her boyfriend to "Please stop," but got a response of "Not yet, I have to come."

Part of me wishes to leave Brooklyn and go back to being a kid. If I picked a time, it'd be that afternoon on a weekday in California when my first grade class and the partner class next door lined up with our parents to take a picture. A few mothers, my own included, had gotten together to make a time capsule. But now, only some of what I can remember about 1989 seems like it was actually worth saving.

Those were the days when economics declared their trickle. The great fall became symbolic of the power of wars waged through cold.

In that photo on the day of the time capsule, my round face smooshed together with the elfin face of a friend who'd go on to give birth to her first baby years before so many other girls experienced a first kiss.

Maybe nothing was ever perfect.

So far, my favorite thing about this new life in this new place, Brooklyn, is that every weekday on the C, 2, or 3 trains, there will be a polo and plaid skirt clique of five or six little black girls riding to school, nodding their heads and belting out popular songs from the radio.

I wonder what kind of grown woman Brooklyn will make me.

SPUTNIK

There was a bar I used to hang out at called Sputnik. It was one block away from the projects, just behind Classon, where teenage boys would stand outside on the sidewalk, loving to call out "Goddamn...god*damn*!" over and over again as soon as the next black honey came by.

To reach Sputnik, we walked to space in the nighttime and the day. Ate French toast and drank German beer in front of the bar's open window. Sat close to cool Brooklyn folk from the factory apartments just across the street. There were black men who dressed like Jimi, and white people who wore thin clothes of cotton like Bob and both Joans.

Together, we were all too young and cool and free to belong to this time or this place.

There was Tony, Latino, deep brown skin and angled eyes. Tony the waiter who lived upstairs and graduated two years before us at our same school. Tony, who wore his hair shaved in the back with the top half pulled up into a shiny black ponytail at the crown of his head. Tony, who brought me French fries and waffles and beer, and for whom I wore a bright blue, flowing skirt and poofed my hair out to copy a peacock. My Tony, who painted on canvas and created animations for film.

My favorite thing about Tony the waiter was the way that his dark brown eyes always flashed when he spoke. And how his mouth was tiny and tidy, but his lips were full like the beautiful beak of a bird.

The downstairs level at Bar Sputnik held an art gallery and performance space.

Once a week men and women came in to watch burlesque. Sometimes hip-hop bands played. Sometimes young comedians told jokes. My friend Ekwa screened two short documentaries there. One film about her father's early life in Kenya and Tanzania. Another about the dollar vans of Brooklyn, where Jamaican and Chinese drivers shuttle folks back and forth, halfway to work. Ekwa, the filmmaker, got married at twenty-seven to her longtime boyfriend, a man who for a living studies the human brain.

At Sputnik, we first saw the work of Angelo, a Brooklyn bartender originally from Indiana who last spring drew one hundred portraits of women's faces. His ex-girlfriend came from Haiti. Her family saw a lot of violence, he once told me while I sat still in his studio space, posed on top of a chair.

My face looked older to him but still young in the cheeks. I saw my neck long like a dancer's. My face tight, like old.

Angelo remains the only man I know in New York who's been violently mugged. This happens to many men, for sure, but he is the only one I know.

Someplace near Bar Sputnik off in Brooklyn late at night, a big woman came at his head with a pipe. She hit his back, and then hit the front of his body.

This Brooklyn lady took Angelo's money, dropped the pipe, and strolled off whistling into the night.

The inside of Sputnik looked like a spaceship. Space like green Martians, flashing rings, and the yellow star of the former U.S.S.R.

Like everywhere else in Brooklyn, none of the furniture at Sputnik matched.

At night, the lampshades beamed their extraterrestrial hue, and come-see-me fliers with red and yellow words and pictures sat stacked on the countertops and pinned against the walls. Like the apartments next door, this space station, my Sputnik, used to be a warehouse too.

What you see most at Sputnik is how hipsters exist at both scenes of Brooklyn, but that us farther South looked different from those on the North. We weren't Hipsterville. We weren't best friends with the crazy daughters of aged rock stars. We didn't believe in the necessity of being cool but rather the necessity of being part of someplace where the real worlds of class, and prejudice, and war, and 9-to-5 outfits that hem well, all do not matter. We were boho in the way of daily escapes into a real fantasyland created by our own hands. We valued above all things else the power and potential of those hands. Angelo's one hundred women. Ekwa's vans. A day begun to indulge in sweetness and beer.

The DJ at Sputnik. The one who dressed like Jimi and wore thin straight-legged pants. His hair was long and brown, in the way that lighter-skinned black people sometimes have, sun-bleached in the way that dreads will become over time. This DJ was colored green and yellow and striped and red. He spun amplified versions of "Crimson and Clover" while my Tony took long smoke breaks then came back inside with no worry as he used sooty hands to serve friends. Sometimes he'd recommend something to read from the bookshelf. The long, multilevel one just near the turntables, where pages lay tattered and covers wore bare.

In petting, there is no Mason-Dixon line.
—Delmore Schwartz

What I remember most about Sputnik was how it'd be hot and muggy all over New York, but cool and breezy in this same boat that we were all in.

THIS WAS ONE

OF MY FRIENDS IN BROOKLYN

I. YUKO.

An evening this weekend in Chinatown at a Vietnamese restaurant with my Japanese friend, Yuko, who is telling me about the Southern collard greens and baked macaroni and cheese dinner that she plans to cook for her black boyfriend at the Thanksgiving holiday. I, in turn, talk about no longer loving the same country boy that I used to, as he's become angry with me over abandoning him for a concert and perhaps other unintentional acts of betrayal that I'll never actually know.

"Forget him," Yuko says. "Go find a *fine brother* anyway." Across the table from me, this woman's face is soft and gorgeous and there's a twinkle on her left nostril from a tiny gem piercing. My friend is five years older. She works in fashion design and strangers often comment that Yuko has got the fullest hips and most ample breasts... Her boyfriend, Raph, now skateboards professionally but when he was a kid used to mule crack for drug dealers in Queens.

"Yuko is going to have black babies," my friend wrinkles up her face confused when she mocks the story of her mother's announcement at a family meal last fall in Japan. All three daughters and the one Japanese son-in-law stayed quiet and kept on eating. Even after the mother's open-ended statement repeated twice, *Yuko is going to have black babies... Yuko is going to have black babies*, not in an angry way or teasing but more in search of a conversation over her unusual fact.

My friend didn't know how to respond to her mother, and didn't really care. Across our restaurant table she makes her face serious and says to me again, "I'm telling you, girlfriend, go get yourself a *good brotha*."

II. WOLF.

{*A lesson about politics, power, race, and representation in America, told to my friend Wolf on his 18th birthday.*}

His father, Israeli: Jews and black Americans, Wolfie. Always vote for candidates who are Jews, and for candidates who are black.

Wolf: Okay...but why?

His father: America does not treat black people very well overall, Wolfie. Always vote so that they gain more representation.

III. NOAH.

Noah, who was kind and honest and came to New York back when he was fourteen and from a small city in Ghana. Last time I saw Noah, he was studying to be a doctor. We last ran into each other on the street.

Me: I'm on my way to buy lunch and just realized that I only have two dollar bills on me.

Noah: Oh no! That's not enough! (Reaches into his own wallet.) Actually, I only have two dollar bills on me too. But take them! At least that way you'll have more to eat.

IV. TAO.

Tao from Texas, my friend who wore remembrance ribbons for Rosa Parks' recent passing on the front of her suit jacket to work at a Midtown hedge fund. Tao is to this day still sending donations to tsunami victims in Sri Lanka, and also started an annual scholarship to benefit one Asian-American girl each year from her Texas hometown.

Me (on the phone with Tao one night): So, how was your day?

Tao: Mad! I finally did it. I called that boy up and said, 'Hey, Eric. You know, I'm walking home right now so late at night in Brooklyn, and it feels a little better when I'm on the phone with someone...' Then, that boy said that he had another call—and never called me back. I could have been raped, stabbed, and robbed, and he never called me back... (Pause.) So, well, how are you?

V. **FABIO**, who wore thick black glasses.

&

SO FAMOUS NOW, with the half sleeve of colorful tattoos.

Fabio, from Italy, was my friend who went to law school by day and worked as a busboy by night. I met him, and the bartender So Famous Now, at the wine spot on Vanderbilt and Prospect, the one that was never quite full of customers but held three walls of bookshelves in its tiny back room.

So Famous Now, the bartender, shared with me a bit about his music and composing. He once stopped me just before the doorway out, with a free take-home bag of chocolate-covered breads.

Fabio, always smiling, sat down next to me one night on the low couch underneath the back-room bookshelves. He set down his busboy's crate of bottles, turned his apron to the side. "Your name sounds the same as the Italian word for 'ax,'" Fabio told me. We wrote *Ascia Vitello* in a page in my notebook.

VI. BEA.

Bea, with the curly black hair. She paid rent in the state of New Jersey but packed overnight bags and preferred to stay at her boyfriend's place out here in the borough of Kings.

One day, riding the C train together, Bea said to me, "I am really unhappy at my job."

So I suggested to her, "You should quit."

And she did.

A different time, Bea and I saw each other at a restaurant while I was out on a blind date. Eighteen inches away, table to table, this is what we said:

Bea: Asha! How you doing? Who's this?

Me: Um...I'm good. This is...Yasha.

Bea: ...

Me: Yes...our names rhyme.

VII. RHONA and CIEL.

Rhona and Ciel, who first met and fell in love at a performance event at the American Indian Community House.

Ciel, half black, worked as a hairstylist high up in a skyscraper in the middle of Manhattan. She told me one day to "Never be dependent on anyone, not even a stylist." And then spent two hours teaching me how to flat iron and curl my own hair.

"Your name sounds the same as the Crow word for river," Rhona once told me while we worked on a history project about the women artists in her hometown. "River woman."

This, is my very favorite story about my friend Rhona:

We used to both know a much older guy, but I won't name him. This man once tried to hold my hand, when no one else was looking, during a fancy party. And every Saturday afternoon while at work (my day off) he bragged to Rhona about how much he loved to cheat on his wife. *Women like Ciel are my type,* this old man once said. *She's gorgeous. What's it like for you when you two have sex?*

My friend Rhona stood up out of her chair.

Rhona, whose grandfather had been a warrior and a chief. Rhona, a visual artist from the days of the old Lower East Side and the old Alphabet City. Rhona, who'd spent her youth on a reservation in Montana, and then spent her first post-Parsons year as a fellow with the Smithsonian in D.C.

Rhona who did not treat the love of her life as an object, or their personal life together as a spectator fantasy.

Rhona stood up.

"OH HELL NO! I DON'T HAVE TO TAKE SHIT OFF OF NO MUTHAFUCKIN MAN!"

And that old guy never said anything else to her again.

VIII. WHAT WAS HIS NAME?

A young man from Nebraska, asked me out for a date one day last winter. We were both so exotic that it felt more lucky than wandering through a grocery store isle of tropical fruits.

This man's body towered high and wide, just slightly less muscular than legend describes the fierce Northern Vikings.

"Wait, you haven't heard any tracks by the Goodie Mob?" Nebraska boy asked me on a Sunday afternoon, thumbing through his home music collection of underground hip-hop and experimental jazz.

"Really, you really don't know how to ice skate? Nebraska?" I asked him a couple of weeks later on a Saturday night, my left arm a crutch weighed down by his 240 pounds as we attempted to glide round the big outdoor rink beside the West Indian Crown Heights.

This very large man's unstrapped belly hung down skinny from his chest like the long pale drop of an old wizard's beard. I once mistook the stretch marks on his upper thighs for tribal tattoos.

Twice he peed into my apartment's toilet without bothering to close the door all the way shut.

We never fell in love.

IX. THE BARTENDER/WAITRESS.

The bartender/waitress, a hip girl from Finland, who for a while worked at my favorite restaurant, Bodega, down on the corner of Fulton Street and Washington Ave.

I cannot remember what we'd say to each other, this friend and I. Sometimes it's true that you only ever remember the way that a person made you feel.

My favorite memory of rebel Finland is the two of us standing together in the night on a corner under a Brooklyn lamppost, waiting for a green signal to cross the street.

Then we jaywalked across that avenue, this girl and I.

I remember that she wore earrings of stars, and together we lit up the night.

X. SANCHEZ.

Sanchez, whose family was from Queens and Colombia. He'd been a history major and knew more about everything than anyone.

This is what happened once when *Xxxx Xxxx* from the Black Panthers came to town to speak:

"Brother *Xxxx*," Sanchez stepped up to a mic in the audience and began. "In these times of war and renewed mistrust, when the government has declared the Patriot Act, and it seems like the government can disregard rights and do whatever it wants, how do we effectively demonstrate? How do we take action?"

Xxxx, who years later would be featured in the magazine *AARP*, said this: "You get your friends, and you get your guns."

Sanchez said thank you and backed away from the mic.

XI. FATIMAH.

It was the daytime and out in Manhattan {because she didn't *do* Brooklyn} when I was walking on the street and out in front of my eyes and feet {because she could conjure herself} appeared Fatimah, a for-real grown ass woman. She walked straight out of a Fifth Avenue hair salon in the middle of the morning on a Tuesday {*Because I have a meeting...*} and reached out to hold my hand while our skirts swished and our heels clicked and we giggled and ran across 14th Street {*Tell me what's going on, dear Asha...I want to hear about you*}. Then she instructed me on three things to do, ways to live life {not telling}. I walked with Fatimah another block to catch a cab {*We will see each other soon, my darling. But now, I am due at the U.N.*}.

XII. DOOLEY.

Dooley was a theater actor I never got the chance to see on stage. He volunteered once a week where I worked, and always wore gentlemen's hats.

My favorite thing Dooley ever said to me:

Him: Last time I was in that neighborhood in Brooklyn, my girlfriend and I were walking past this lady out on her front stoop... and we realized, 'Whoa! It's Joie Lee!' So we said, 'Hi!' Then she talked with us about acting and film for nearly twenty minutes.

Me: ...Who?

Him: Whoa! Are you kidding?! Spike Lee's sister!

XIII. THE YOUNGER SON FROM DOWNSTAIRS.

"Lil' Kim is on the block!" this very sweet, thirteen-year-old Muslim boy once informed me. Down our shared stairwell he ran...hyped for a view of Big Mamma Thang.

"I think she starts serving her year in jail three days from now," I called after him.

"Then come on! We'd better hurry!" this very sweet neighbor called back in reply.

XIV. BENJI.

Two conversations, one year apart.

> *Benji*: How you been doing, lady?
> *Me*: I'm busy, you know. Busy.
> *Benji*: Nah, not all that. I mean, how's your soul?

One year later...

> *Me*: I want to retire at thirty-five and move to a house in the woods.
> *Benji*: Do you know how to use a shotgun?
> *Me*: I'll be safe. I'll get a dog.
> *Benji*: Dog can't kill a bear.

I REMEMBER—

XV. ZOE.

"I'm totally committed to making as much art as possible in the next year," she once said.

Zoe showed me her female orgasm series and shared memories of her father's monthly salon for Latin American artists.

Together we'd walk the streets and discuss the challenges for developing as a young woman artist.

XVI. ANTHONY A.

He was my first friend in Brooklyn to buy his own home, earned by years of working as a night manager from ten at night to six a.m., paying for school and saving the rest of his money.

One night when he was off work, we hung out and watched *The Color Purple.*

The busiest guy I knew, Anthony also played the trumpet, and was a conductor for a nationally ranked Brooklyn marching band.

XVII. MARIAM.

My friend the schoolteacher. We once took off outside on a sunshiny day in the middle of the afternoon to go play in the park.

Whiffle ball. Big red bat. Broken kite.

XVIII. IAN.

Three years older. He once called me from his cell phone as he stood on the sidewalk next to my building's front door.

"Been hanging out in your neighborhood. Hung over..." It was another sunny afternoon, perhaps the brightest of the year. So we walked and took an hour to reach the canal.

XIX. AMIE.

Who was half Thai, and liked to jokingly refer to her white father as "round eye."

XX. GIA.

The only person I know who's worked at *National Enquirer.*

Neither she nor I had health insurance for the same period of about three years.

"The Internet said I had gonorrhea," one of us said to the other. "But it turned out to just be pink eye."

XXI. ALLISON.

With whom I once shared a bedroom, and a bed, at a white-walled mansion in Miami. This was the last, and fanciest, slumber party of my adult life.

XXII. RODNEY (a woman).

Of the very rare Brooklyn tribes of:
1. Young women opera singers
2. Very long golden hair

When I was out of a job once, Rodney found me two.

XXIII. JASE.

Originally from Houston, and whose first language wasn't English, so he had to learn it in neighborhood schools on that city's Southwest side.

One Brooklyn night very late, Jase sat next to me on a rooftop.

So, this is life? we asked the stars.

A STORY

Once upon a time on Fulton Street, a broken-nose boy originally from the sticks out West trialed far one night, six Brooklyn blocks down and one avenue over, to visit that first apartment with the bedroom without a window. That nose pushed forward and left behind obstacles of the men hunched in prayer, the man-boy who brayed, and so many shoes to scare away anyone practical. The boy carried in a cloth sack no weapon more than one plastic container of cut and sweetened apples rested next to dough.

My maiden eyes watched that broken nose knead piecrust with fingertips and hold fruit syrup in his palm. My curved back became flat at the press of his whole chest, and cinnamon dampness steeped between both of our shirts.

That first year in the kingdom of Brooklyn, a thousand little looking glasses relinquished all vocal power and stopped telling their grown woman beholders what not to see.

A mouth ripe to nonpoisonous apples. Eyelids shuttered open by a broken nose.

II. This Was My Mama / 1988 through 2000

As a small child, the rules of race confused me. This was largely due to a conflict of ideology between most of the rest of the world, and my mother.

One Fourth of July when I am eight and she is forty, I ask my mother to tell me stories about America's founding fathers and our Uncle Sam, that man in the red and white, up and down striped hat.

"Independence Day for whom?" My mother answers me fast. She has dark skin like mine and hair pinned up in a messy twist with bangs and loose pieces. My mother wears dresses and makeup, dark lipstick and rouge on her face. Her look is perfect late eighties.

"Sweetheart, today is not our day. Sam is not our uncle. Not everyone was free."

We buy fireworks from a local vendor and explode them in our front driveway, eating ketchup-laden hot dogs with another family of non-freedom celebratory friends. Two moms and two kids. It's nighttime. A man walks by on the street with his daughter who appears to be close to my age. The pair is black like all of us. The man says hello to my mother and they begin a friendly conversation. He invites his way into our fireworks celebration and she allows him, offering the girl a hot dog and chips, giving her father sparklers to light and hold up in front of his child.

My mother likes to do nice things for all children. In the daytime her job is for the county as a social worker. My mother has told me about the work that she does. She feels sad when she has to take babies out of houses where their parents don't take good care of them. She acted tough the time that she walked into an apartment and saw a group of men with black tears marked on their faces, and number 13s marked on their hard necks. The time when men who had bright red faces and smooth pale heads, and were much larger than she is, called her names and threatened fist fights. Last week my mother bought a new bicycle for a boy whose own mother works as a prostitute.

Tonight, at our fireworks party, we touch matches to tiny blue and pink cylinders that whistle like banshee spirits and smell worse than the burning charcoal on our grill. The new man takes over most of the lighting and running, while the rest of us *ooh* and *ahh* and watch a million popping and fading colors.

"I love this holiday," the man says.

"Just for fun, not in reverence," Mom leans over to remind me.

Halloween comes in one week. I am invited to trick or treat with another girl from school but I know that my mother will say *No*.

"Would we go begging any other day of the year?" she states more than asks the question to me one evening at dinnertime, over seasoned lamb and a broccoli vegetable, after I bring it up. "Well would we? No." I decide in my head that when I am older and grown, my own children can trick or treat if they want to.

Mom drives us to the store and buys three supersized bags of gummy candies for me to eat whenever I want. Mom buys one bag of

M&M's and one bag of Chick-O-Sticks for herself. We start into the candy bags in the car. She is a little bit chubby now, more than when I was younger, but has always been beautiful and fond of wearing stylish clothes.

My mother, the lucky one, every day puts on overcoats of cloth that are dark-colored like slippery leaves from the side of a nature trail, thick to touch like the royal skin of an eggplant. These coats flow like robes and show swirl and sparkle designs.

My mother is stardust rising and falling whenever she waves an arm.

My mother plays with costumes every day of the year.

On this Halloween night, my mother drops me off for a few hours to take part in a Harvest celebration at a local, black Baptist church.

Nearly two hundred other disappointed kids sing songs about Jesus and play carnival games. We memorize Bible verses for candy. There is hay in the building that makes me sneeze.

When she returns, my mother asks lots of questions about how the evening went.

"A deacon helped me to bob for apples. He had on a farmer's hat and blue jean overalls."

Although we are not normally churchgoing, she seems quite pleased.

The next year for Halloween, I ask my mother if I may dress up as a vampire.

"Satanic," she tells me.

A mobster?

"Negative. Violent. That's not how you want to represent yourself." She buys me a black baseball cap that we find hanging on a hook at our local drugstore, and together, my mother and I pick out the thickest and longest straight-hair ponytail from a beauty supply shop that's two neighborhoods away from ours. At a costume seller in the middle of our city's downtown, we are able to find a small, gold-colored earring that's shaped like a key. My mother, for this one night only, applies bold lines of grown-up makeup to my puffy nine-year-old face.

"I am Janet Jackson from the *Rhythm Nation* tour," I explain to all the other kids and a few supervising parents at Kendra K's Halloween slumber party. "Monster Mash" plays in the background and little kids drink punch out of orange plastic cups and eat chocolate chip cookies on bat-decorated napkins.

The Janet Jackson pop star costume is her idea, my mother's. I love it and make a big show to all of the other kids of doing jerky dance movements whenever possible, and occasionally jogging in place with my arms held out stiff.

Superman, Sleeping Beauty, and a witch girl all watch but do not get excited.

Just before bedtime when I am no longer cool-girl-Janet but back to regular me in fuchsia pajamas, Mrs. Kojima helps me take off the hair tie around my long black ponytail and shrieks when the bundle of hair falls off into her hands.

"Is this what your mother wears too, dear?" she asks.

My mother loves Christmastime more than any other holiday. At the end of every year, the house smells of ginger and pine. We spend a little bit of time every night of the Christmas season that I am six adding brown angel dolls to the pointy limbs of a tree that reaches up to the ceiling. Angels with brown faces, and dressed in red and gold, hover on bookcases, windowsills, and ledges in every room. These small protectors make up my mother's favorite collection.

One evening closer to the holiday, my mother places plastic light-up versions of Santa and Mrs. Claus just beside our dark brick fireplace near the tall tree. Their faces illuminate through brown plastic. Their bodies burn tomato red.

At school for an art project I color in a black outline of Santa. His face, like on the plastic model at my home, gets colored brown. His beard becomes black. The red and white suit is standard. Mrs. Garcia, our teacher who is old and married to the president of the city's school board, instructs us to "Wrap it up, because art time is over!" I walk to the back of the room to turn in my picture of Santa, and I stop to look at everyone else's. All the other Santas are white.

KJ is the black boy in my class. KJ's little brown body still carries baby fat. His mother likes to dress him in sideways striped shirts of black and neon green.

I search through all the Santa papers until I find one with KJ's initials. His Santa has peach skin too.

Maybe my mother is wrong.

I hide my Santa underneath KJ's paper.

Mom picks me up from school in the gray Volvo and we drive the five minutes to home. I am awfully quiet, so she asks what's wrong.

"What color is Santa?" I want to know. Then my mother is awfully quiet, but for less than one minute.

"What color is your father?" she smiles and asks me back.

"He is black," I answer.

"Okay then," Mom says. "That's what color Santa is too." We both smile, content.

My mother is not trying to be revolutionary or political, just to make everything make sense for me.

After that year, every Christmas from the time I am six on until I move away, some friend from school will come over to our house, drink my mother's spiced cider, and get into a debate with her about our ever-growing collection of black Santa figures. The angels are always, "Oh, so pretty," but a chocolate Santa that's not made out of candy apparently seems foolhardy and contentious.

"He was white and from Germany," a friend who is blond says one year. My mother ignores this person and speaks to me.

"Tell honey that your father is black and from L.A."

ALL FEET NO HANDS

(A SOCCER PLAYER'S MOST MEMORABLE

BASKETBALL GAME)

Preseason, 1995.
Seventh grade.
A whistle blows.

Coach Joe casts a sidelong glance to his left on the bench. The man's hair sparks red like fire and his eyes, though dark brown, blaze equally as bright. Coach Joe has a face that scrunches up and projects intensity in the manner of an incited Popeye.

"Veal, 22!!!" Coach Joe bellows jockish and deep, commanding action without any further verbal order or facial expression.

Veal 22 raises up off of her haunches. Her FILA kicks sparkle brand-new, not at all dingy or scuffed. They are that new high-top white pair with the reflective navy stripe that outlines each side of the shoe's street-boot shape. Hey, those shoes are cool, *the boys in school had a few weeks earlier told her, which granted 22 a cross-gender comaraderie and made the blue-rimmed FILAs tolerably OK. Before, she'd hated those shoes.* Rock my Adidas, *22 had thought. Her* mother made her wear the shoes, purchased from the young men's footwear section at Costco.

"Get'cha head in the game!!!" Joe calls out as 22 sprints onto the court, a thin gold ribbon holding a black ponytail in place.

FILAs and a hair ribbon.

She slaps hands with her teammates, older girls, already out on the floor.

"Let's go babe," someone else's father calls. It's Mr. Dominguez. Annie's father, who used to be a cop. Mr. Dominguez is very kind to all the kids, and will die unexpectedly two years later from a lung problem.

Mr. Dominguez smiles and claps encouragingly. He's someone you always remember, because he was there for all the kids.

Another whistle blows. The herd of pre-teenage girl warriors moves together up and then back down the court. They're all under a basket, jumping up and down on springs, while tall Christy catches three of her own rebounds and then succeeds in scoring. The other team throws in. The new ball holder stands in 22's zone.

This is it.

22 attacks the girl's back like a sudden, hairy spider that's been unexpectedly violated. Arms aggressive and everywhere, face ugly and hissing. The ball holder is trapped and stunned, bewildered as to where to find an out or turn.

"Foul, 22!" A referee calls.

"That was awesome!" Someone else's parent, or perhaps one of the watching teachers calls out. "What a great foul. She went right over that girl's back!"

Once, just a few months prior in a soccer game, 22 ran at an opposing player and collided with the girl, making the thin skin just below the girl's left knee bleed. Another time she banged faces in an airborne triangle, after going up against two other players at the same time for a header.

All three briefly blacked out.

22 never felt responsible, or cared. She knew about and felt comfortable playing soccer, even with groups of boys.

She was the girl in the sixth grade that when she walked up to the kickball diamond, the other kids knew to move farther back.

But this was seventh grade, and basketball.

And to this day, 22 still wants to know: **What the hell kind of game stops play for such a tiny foul?**

III. Everyone Gets a War / 2005 and 2001

At the end of last spring, two military boys my same age flew out of Iraq and landed at a rooftop party (not Brooklyn) in New York.

Yup, active combat in Iraq. We've just been here, off of Fort Brag, two days.

One soldier, his dark eyes flashed on a thin but handsome face. His teeth were small and square. Dog tags hung down from around his neck. This soldier made a good time for himself by playing barkeep to all the women, sliding his agile legs from one end to the other of a freestanding countertop. This soldier's hips teased, hypnotic, like string held up in front of cats. An artsy girl with long brown hair and solid black tights won out to join him as the evening's partner in laughing.

The soldier's dessert arm stayed slung over the artsy girl's navy shoulders all night long. She in turn held tight to his belted waist. Together the new pair sipped out of wine glasses, brandished cigarettes during conversation, and laughed and smiled bigger than his small mouth with small teeth seemed able. He and she guffawed like haughty aristocrats, giggled like kids on a playground, hooted like sport teammates witnessing a locker-room prank.

This soldier put on a drama of normalcy. She was a USO hire excited to welcome in the troops.

And the other soldier, blond buzz cut and thick muscles, he knocked into my right-side shoulder and thudded against a wall. This boy grew up working-class in Texas. He didn't talk much and walked through the evening alone with a bottle of beer.

When I was younger and learning about history, I never imagined I'd also grow up to be at parties where there were guys coming home from war.

EVERYONE GETS A WAR
II

From: asha*******@yahoo.com {age 19}
To: j**********@hotmail.com
Subject:
Date: Thu, 13 Sept 2001 11:57:15 (PDT)

Tuesday morning, just after nine, I was startled awake by the rocking of our thirty-story residence building. The building rocked HARD, but moved quickly back into place.

Heidi, one of the suitemates in our apartment on the fourteenth floor, ran into my bedroom and said that she thought she'd felt an earthquake.

Laleh, my roommate was still asleep. Jenna, our other suitemate, was already on campus at an early class.

So I got out of bed and walked into our living room to join Heidi, seeing on the televsion screen that two planes had just flown through the Twin Towers of the World Trade Center, blocks away from our Water Street residence hall.

Laleh's mother called, frantic, to ask if we were safe. Not anticipating the chaos to come, I promised that we wouldn't walk outside to look at the towers' damage, and said that we were all fine.

Immediately after, a high school friend from California called our apartment to ask about our safety. I said yes again, and asked this friend to please call my parents and let them know. After hanging up, and then attempting to dial out again, the phone lines in our building went down. We could no longer make any outgoing calls, or accept incoming calls.

Laleh woke up, and together the three girls in our suite continued to watch the news, with no understanding that the planes had been part of an attack.

Then, after seeing images and reports from Washington, D.C., and Pennsylvania, we understood.

I suggested going out to a store to buy emergency supplies. Things like water, dry and canned food, and flashlights. Laleh agreed to go too, and Heidi agreed to stay inside in case the phones started working, and to keep watching the news. But Laleh wanted to have breakfast before going out, and it seems odd now to have been eating toast and honey while looking outside the living room window and seeing perhaps thousands of people walking across the Brooklyn Bridge all at once.

After nearly twenty minutes, Laleh and I took the elevator downstairs to go to a bank and grocery store, both a short walk to the west.

At the lobby, it seemed as if the warning group of students was waiting for us. Twelve people began screaming to go back up to our apartment and close the vents and windows. One of the towers had just collapsed.

Back on fourteen, we ran into two friends and as a small group decided that it wasn't safe so high in a building. Heidi knew someone on the third floor, so we headed down the stairwell.

Other students came onto the stairwell at the landing of every floor, all together trying to get low or get out of the building. No one yelled though, and no one panicked.

John, from the third floor, didn't answer the door when we arrived at his room. Heidi heard later that he'd been directly across the street when the first plane hit. He saw, and then took the A train—the very last before that subway line temporarily shut-down—back up to campus at West 4th Street.

Heidi knocked on a door across the hall and a stranger, Pat, let us in with him and his roommate, a volunteer firefighter. A thick cloud of dust outside had darkened the view outside from Pat's living room.

We all sat together and watched the TV. My friends showed a mix of emotions: some cried, some made jokes, some worried about family in D.C. Pat sat silent with rage, and his roommate couldn't sit at all, so angry and wanting to go outside to work with the other firefighters.

That's when we all felt a strong rumble, and then saw the news reporter onscreen. The second tower had fallen. A second giant cloud of smoke and debris began to roll forward. The reporter and news crew started to run.

The windows outside Pat and the volunteer firefighter's room became completely dark.

We'd have to evacuate downtown Manhattan, is what a resident adviser yelled and knocked on the door. I asked Pat to borrow a shirt to put over my face.

By the time I reached the lobby dowstairs, I couldn't find my friends. I begged a maintenance person from the building to let me look in his key closet to find the extra set for my room. I wanted to go back up to the apartment. Laleh had been carrying my asthma inhaler in her bag, and I needed to grab another.

Althea, a resident advisor in the lobby, volunteered to walk back upstairs with me. We got the inhaler, a backpack, and my wallet, and I changed from sandals to sneakers before we headed out.

Outside, the dark cloud had subsided, but the worst thing was trying to keep dust out of our eyes. All around, people covered in dust were walking uptown, not going any particular place.

We saw a man trying to cover his face with a coffee filter.

Still, no one we saw panicked.

Restaurants and the seaport's fish markets, these local businesses opened their doors early to offer people cups of water to drink and hoses to use to wash off.

By the time Althea and I reached Canal Street, the air seemed more breathable. We kept walking to campus. The walk took us an hour, or maybe much more. I hadn't thought to keep track, and couldn't tell.

Althea and I separated, and I looked for my friends.

At the campus sports center, food and mats were set out for students who'd come from downtown or evacuated. The building would be used as a student shelter. I stayed there, hoping to eventually see my friends. I did see a few other girls I knew, who'd had to leave their Chinatown dorm as well, and we sat together.

Soon, Laleh arrived with another friend, Katie. Laleh had waited for me outside of our residence building, but eventually had to flee.

Laleh and Katie invited me to leave, to Brooklyn, to all stay together at an older friend's apartment. Heidi was still missing, but likely fine. Before the group split, she mentioned wanting to go up to Spanish Harlem to stay with a friend.

The F train was operating again, and free to ride, but all the Brooklyn-bound trains were packed solid. After letting five trains pass, we finally pushed onto one. Even then, we barely made it.

Brooklyn, was so quiet and peaceful. I was able to call home. My mom told me that Jenna, who we hadn't seen all day, was heading home to Long Island and that it had been arranged for me to meet her at Penn Station to go with her.

I had to go back into the city, alone, but found Jenna easily. I felt safe with a best friend, and we took the train to Long Island.

I've been with Jenna and her family since Tuesday night. They are very nice people and I am comfortable here. There's a bed for me in the guest room, but I don't want to sleep alone so am sharing with Jenna in hers. Even with everything going on, it's a bit funny because she kicks at night.

In this neighborhood on Long Island, it's peaceful and almost like nothing has happened. But we watch the news all day on television.

School will resume on Monday. Most of the student housing will be open, but not our dorm because it's so close. Jenna's mom said that we can stay for a while at her uncle's guesthouse on Staten Island, because it's closer to school, if we need to. Our dorm building may collapse from shaken foundation, or it may be crushed when other buildings around it start to fall. There are lots of rumors going around, but really, no one knows.

Being downtown that morning, everything felt awful. I do not wish this feeling on anyone anywhere, not ever. It seems like this is what many other people around the world are forced to experience often, and how so many people live and what they go through every day. This should not go on. This should happen to no one.

NOTES

Opening quote taken from: Jones, Hettie. Telephone interview. 23 March, 2007.

about the author

Asha Veal Brisebois' published work as a writer and editor has been acquired in libraries and collections including the George Gustav Heye Center at the Smithsonian Institution's National Museum of the American Indian, University of Toronto Libraries, Museum Volkenkunde (Leiden, Netherlands), and others. Her work in creative nonfiction has been published by Brooklyn-based Slice Literary, among others. She is the founder of The Places We've Been books / The Places We've Been LLC, working since 2011 with more than 48 writers from cities and countries including London, Greece, Tanzania, Dubai, Lebanon, Montreal, Vancouver, South Africa, Scotland, Paris, New York, Los Angeles, Chicago, and more; with their affiliations and honors from the National Endowment for the Arts, BBC, StoryCorps, Marvel, MTV Base, The New York Times, and more. In 2013 she published *The Places We've Been: Field Reports from Travelers Under 35*, which received acknowledgment from the Illinois Humanities Council; and has been added to syllabi for college and university courses in cultural anthropology, Africana studies, and creative writing. In 2006 she edited *Apsaalooke: Art & Tradition*, which now resides in collections including the Smithsonian. Asha graduated from New York University, and the MFA program at The New School.

CPSIA information can be obtained at www.ICGtesting.com
Printed in the USA
LVOW10*0236060815

449010LV00002B/4/P